THE FOUNDATION OF THE WORLD: A SHORT INTRODUCTION TO THE THEOLOGY OF ORIGEN

Jonathan McCormack

ABOUT THIS BOOK

Origen wrote in Greek, yet *On First Principles* survives only as an elaborated Latin translation by Rufinus that contains indications of having been considerably altered.

There's much controversy on how to structure *On First Principles*. This introduction to Origen's theology is drawn from Fr. John Behr's translation and Reader's Edition of *On First Principles*,[i] which is structured differently than the previous English translations of this work. Many theological points are not included in this book because they are basic Christian doctrines now taken for granted or else refutations of obscure heresies and pagan beliefs that have little relevance for modern readers.

This book, rather, includes five overarching themes that are important to Origen and will be most relevant to modern readers: the Incarnation, scripture, Creation, the fall, and eschatology. They are ordered to reflect the beginning and the culmination of Origen's perspective.

These themes follow after an important introduction to Origen and to *On First Principles*.

ABOUT ORIGEN

Origen of Alexandria (185-254) is considered the first systematic Christian theologian.[1] However, there is a great deal of controversy about what he actually taught and believed. This is due to unsubstantiated rumors as well as to alterations of his original text. Besides this, he is a complicated thinker.

Panayiotis Tzamalikos tells us that Origen 's teacher was likely Ammonius, who taught Plotinus.[ii] Tzamalikos says Origen probably converted to Christianity in his 50s, and his conversion scandalized the Greeks. Although Origen was certainly influenced by Plato, Tzamalikos insists that Origen was no Platonist; indeed, much of Origen's writings

---

[1] Except where otherwise cited, the information in this introduction can be found in Fr. John Behr's edition of *On First Principles*.

explicitly argue against Platonic teachings that denigrate matter and embodied existence. Origen is unique in that he was attacked both by Christians, for being too Platonic, and by pagans, for being a Christian. Origen was the first Christian to speak of three "hypostases" (or persons) in the Trinity and to use the term "homoousios"[2] for the relation between the Father and the Son.

Many rumors about Origen were likely just that. He almost certainly did not castrate himself. Origen was a rock star in the ancient world. When someone's theology was in doubt, Origen was sent to investigate. He even taught the faith to the Empress Mamaea. According to Eusebius,[iii] Origen's father was martyred for the faith when Origen was just a teenager, and during the massacre of Christians later launched by Decius, Origen himself, by then in his 60s, suffered extreme torture, being stretched on the rack. Eusebius says Origen spent his final days as a broken man, writing letters "full of comfort to those in need," until his death a few years later. Though historians regard Eusebius's account to be rather dubious, they agree that Origen was persecuted towards the end of his life for his Christian faith.

---

[2] Homoousios, or "consubstantial" in English, means "one in being" or "of the same substance."

ABOUT *ON FIRST PRINCIPLES*

Most of Origen's writings have not survived. Among those that have, *On First Principles*, written around 220-230 AD, is his most famous and his most controversial. Even so, his other writings were highly valued. St Jerome, who venomously criticized *On First Principles*, extolled Origen's commentary on the Song of Songs and also called Origen "the greatest teacher of the Churches next to the Apostles."[iv]

The Philokalia, most beloved by Christians, features large compilations of Origen's works, assembled by the Cappadocian Fathers St. Basil and St. Gregory Nazianzus.[v]

Origen was beloved by many saints. St. Athanasius and St. Pamphilus, for example, both defended Origen in his lifetime. Origen converted St. Ambrose to Christianity from Gnostic Valentinianism. He was highly influential to St. Basil and St. Gregory of Nyssa. St. Gregory Nazianzen called Origen "the whetstone of us all.[vi] Hans Urs von Balthasar said that "there is no thinker in the church who is so invisibly all-present as Origen."[vii]

Indeed, Origen was the first to attempt a systematic Christian theology. He defines Christian beliefs in his preface to *On First*

Principles,[3] which closely approximates what would later be contained in the Nicene Creed. That is all he teaches as dogmatically true. For the rest, he is only giving his opinions and speculations. He submits his teachings to the church and explicitly states that if anything he teaches is found to contradict either the scriptures or the church, or if anyone discovers a better interpretation, the reader ought to dismiss what he has erroneously taught.

A controversial question often posed is: Was Origen anathematized?

The answer is complicated. In Origen's lifetime, much of Orthodox theology was still being worked out. Origen was teaching before the formulation of the Nicene Creed and before dogmas were officially laid down, and the council that supposedly anathematized him, the Second Council of Constantinople, came centuries after his death.

The Second Council of Constantinople in 553 (the Fifth Ecumenical Council) mentions Origen by name and states that those who teach his doctrines are to be anathematized.

However, the 15 anathemas against "Origenism" traditionally attributed to this

---

[3] Read Origen's preface to *On First Principles* at www.newadvent.org/fathers/04120.htm

council (which don't name Origen himself) are today questioned by historians. Church historian Norman P. Tanner's 1990 edition of the *Decrees of the Ecumenical Councils* does not include the anti-Origenist denunciations, stating that "recent studies have shown that these anathemas cannot be attributed to this council."[viii] Additionally, Metropolitan Kallistos Ware explains there is "considerable doubt whether these fifteen anathemas were in fact formally approved by the Fifth Ecumenical Council. They may have been endorsed by a lesser council, meeting in the early months of 553 shortly before the main council was convened, in which case they lack full ecumenical authority..."[ix]

Many historians believe these anathemas were secretly added later by Emperor Justinian without the bishops' knowledge. The Orthodox historian and theologian Fr. John Anthony McGuckin explains, "The anathemata did not get themselves attached to the official acts of the council of 553, but...were quietly added to the synodal acts at a later date... a sleight of hand made possible by those who held the key to the archives."[x]

At best, the Emperor Justinian may have submitted the anathemas to the bishops after the council. Yet even if the bishops approved of the anathemas, the anathemas cannot, without being part of the council, be said to possess canonical authority.

In addition, it has become universally accepted that these anathemas and reports of Justinian were directed primarily against sixth-century "Origenism" rather than against Origen himself. This "Origenism" was heavily influenced by Gnosticism and had little to do with Origen's actual teachings. In fact, Origen frequently defended the faith against the Gnostics. According to Tzamilikos, Justinian had no knowledge at all of Origen's actual writings, and, at the time, the term "Origenism" was a catch-all phrase for anything or anyone that threatened the ecclesiastical authorities.

Still, one shouldn't gloss over the fact that Origen was a controversial figure even in his own lifetime. And future ecumenical councils would affirm the previous condemnations of Origenism, regardless of whether they were acquainted with his actual texts and teachings.

According to the understanding of several respected Origen scholars including Fr. John Behr, Marguerite Harl,[xi] Mark Julian Edwards,[xii] and Panayiotis Tzamalikos,[xiii] Origen does not believe in the pre-existence of souls or in reincarnation. A belief that *is* attributed to Origen is universalism. Further explanation of these points is below.

A PERFECT CREATION IN ETERNITY

Origen did not teach the pre-existence of souls. What he *did* teach is that God always had the intention of a perfect creation, which always exists outside of time, in eternity. We exist as fleshly beings because we are intended by God to become perfected, to become that which, in eternity, we always are. Those who make it to heaven are, in some sense, always already there. That is why the Bible uses odd phrases, such as that something "will be" and "already is."

As David Bentley Hart states, "Because we were all of us... before the foundations of the world, called into existence in the heavenly court; there, in the eternal intention and perfected creation of God, we are already—and in that sense eternally have ever been—joined to God, pervaded by his glory like iron thrust into the fire."[xiv]

Origen scholar Marguerite Harl points out that the terms that appear in G. W. Butterworth's translation of Origen's *On First Principles*, "the pre-existence of souls," "pre-existent souls," and "préexistent intellects," do not actually occur in the writings of Origen.[xv] Origen specifically argued against the Platonic conception that immaterial souls fell into bodies here on earth. As early as the third century, St. Pamphilus in his *Apology for Origen*[xvi] attests that Origen was wrongly accused of maintaining the preexistence of souls falling into bodies.

For Origen, as for most of the ancients, only God can be said to be without a body. Even the "bodiless powers," according to St. John of Damascus, is a relative term; angels indeed have bodies, though ones much subtler than our own. So, there can be no such thing as a mere bodiless soul.

WORLDS, AEONS, ETERNAL CREATION, AND REINCARNATION

Origen speaks of different worlds. Many interpret Origen to mean literal various worlds, as in different planets. However, Fr. John Behr seems to interpret him using "world" and "age" as a period characterized by a certain way of life and understanding. For example, we speak of the "Iron Age" or the "Roman world." And when speaking of eternity, Origen likely meant many "ages" in which we will become prepared to forever grow in love and likeness to God.

The word "aeon" was used in many ways in the ancient world. St. John of Damascus, for example, used "aeon" as "eschatological time," the time without end that characterizes the age to come.[xvii] For Origen, a system of aeons is a complex system of educational institutions, and the world's history is a long educational process directing the whole universe to salvation. The aeons can be thought of as vertical spheres of a specific kind of space-time matrix. The "higher" up the realm, the more spiritual it is and the closer it is to God. David Bentley Hart notes that in the New Testament, "...it is best to imagine the aeons not as successive eras along a single 'horizontal' causal trajectory, but rather as spheres of being rising 'vertically' to the threshold of the divine realm 'beyond all ages.'"[xviii]

Origen does not believe in reincarnation.[xix] Origen explicitly refutes all Egyptian, Greek, Pythagorean, and Platonic notions of reincarnation or transformation. No one is "born twice," and there is no disembodied soul that incarnates into different bodies. Neither can a spiritual body exist in different aeons. Neither will a human soul ever "descend" into an animal body or into another creature. A soul is always embodied.[4]

Origen does not believe in an eternal creation. This cosmos had a beginning and will one day perish.

---

[4] See also Wohrer, "Pop Patristic Reincarnation?" and Ramelli, "The Christian Doctrine of Apokatastasis," 728.

UNIVERSALISM

Origen taught universalism. He wrote that everyone would be saved, according to Paul's word that one day Christ will be "all in all."[xx] Origen did believe in hell, but he considered it temporary and purgative.

The kind of universalism specifically denounced by the Fifth Ecumenical Council was not the version Origen actually taught. St. Isaac the Syrian and St. Gregory of Nyssa also taught universalism, yet they were not anathematized. However, most Orthodox Christians throughout history have considered universalism heretical.

SCRIPTURE

One of the greatest things we can learn from Origen is how to read the Bible.

Scripture is an inspired text with which we can commune with God. You can't do that with a history book! This doesn't deny the historical aspects; this just means these historical events carry a spiritual meaning and that God can communicate to us through a story, whether the story is factual or not.

The great Jewish Biblical scholar James Kugel reminds us that the ancients read scripture according to four principles. First, scripture must have its meaning revealed. The plain meaning must be "opened," as Christ opened the scriptures to the Apostles on the road to Emmaus. Second, scripture's purpose is not to inform us about events in the past but about events in the present. That means the story of Jonah is about, among other things, what's happening *right now*. For example, perhaps the whale is a particular sin that is coming for you because you are running from it. Third, scripture is harmonious; it contains no contradictions. Fourth, scripture is inspired by the Holy Spirit, who in Christ speaks to us directly.

Recall that Origen begins with Christ crucified. Therefore, Origen reads scripture through the cross, as all the church fathers did. This is the "eschatological" reading. Eschatology is the end; it is the revealing. On the cross, Jesus is revealed as God. This is what Origen calls the "spiritual meaning" of scripture, as opposed to the fleshly meaning. For example, Christ on the cross appears as a mere man to fleshly eyes. But His true divine nature is revealed at His crucifixion, where we finally see not just a man, but God Himself.

Without the revelation of Christ, the Old Testament can tell only a shadow of the Truth. The apostles knew the scriptures but could not recognize Christ as God until after His passion on the cross.

This means that everything in the Old Testament must refer to Christ. For example, the church fathers will say Moses is a type of Christ. Moses goes into Egypt, which represents death, and through the Red Sea, which represents baptism, and is "resurrected" when he is led to the promised land, which refers to heaven. The story of Moses really refers to Christ crucified and risen! Origen will say that, without the cross, the Old Testament is only myth, even if it happened. St Gregory of Nyssa agreed: "Therefore, the Apostle said, 'the letter kills, but the spirit gives life,' since often if we were to stand in the mere concrete reality of the history, scripture would offer us no patterns at all of the good life."[xxi]

The following introduction to Origen's theology explains Origen's thought from *On First Principles* on the Incarnation, scripture, Creation, the fall, and eschatology, themes which, for Origen, are interwoven. It is written in the first-person tense, as if Origen is explaining them to modern readers.

THE FOUNDATION OF THE WORLD: A SHORT INTRODUCTION TO THE THEOLOGY OF ORIGEN

THE INCARNATION

God cannot be known to us in His essence, or *ousia.* Rather He is known by His *dunamis,* or power. It is His power that acts upon other beings. God's power is infinite and mediated by the second person of the Trinity, who is Jesus Christ. Christ is Himself the visible image of the invisible God.

The world was created through Jesus Christ.[xxii] Christ is that divine helpmate who declares in Proverbs 8:22 that the Lord created her in the beginning of His ways. We must be careful however; the verb "created" in this text does not imply that the Son has a temporal beginning.

Jesus lays down his soul of His own accord during the Passion. He is the lamb, and He is slain. This happens in time at a particular place and moment, but its reality is ever-present in eternity. This is why Jesus's soul, along with His flesh, is called the Son of God. On the cross He becomes, within time, that which He always *is* in eternity: the Son of God.

Christ becomes in time what He is in eternity, so that through Him we might do the same. His soul, though no different from others, wills the Word of God so perfectly that this will becomes His nature. Thus, our human nature can now too be home to the Holy Spirit.

Since we are all created to be partakers of the heavenly liturgy in eternity,[5] our true selves are in some profound sense already united with God; "hidden with Christ in God," as Colossians puts it.

Before His passion, the apostles could only see Christ as a mere man; they saw his fleshly properties only. However, in the light of His passion, they saw that He was both human and divine.

His death on the cross is the fullest revelation of God! On the cross, with the flesh crucified, we can finally see God as He is. We must dare to say that the goodness of Christ appeared greater, more divine, and truly in accordance with the image of the Father when He humbled Himself and became obedient unto death. God is most revealed when He is crucified, for the shape of love itself is cruciform and sacrificial.

When Christ was exalted on the cross, human nature itself was exalted by mingling with the infinite nature of God. You see, the lowliness of Jesus in the flesh was raised up with the Father's glory. This is how He became Lord instead of servant, Christ the King instead

---

[5] Sverre Elgvin Lied's book *Participation in Heavenly Worship* explores early Christians' understanding of their participation, with angels and saints, in the eternal liturgy of heaven.

of a subject, highest instead of lowly.

Those who say the Son was merely a man and was then adopted by the Father are in error. The church affirms that Jesus Christ was and is always the God-man in eternity. For what is always in eternity appeared in time on the cross to us. And what is Jesus Christ in eternity? Perfect God and perfect man, perfectly together. He slain from the foundation of the world.

There was never a time when Jesus Christ was not fully divine and fully human.[6] The Incarnation is not an event in the life of some pre-incarnate divinity who then descends into fleshly life, only to suffer death on a cross, and thereafter to return to its preferred pre-Incarnate condition. For just as the Son is eternally begotten of the Father, so the Word is eternally Incarnate.

God exists in eternity, which has no time. God does not have a "life story" such that the Incarnation in Christ only happens to God at some particular time and place. And since the Incarnation always already includes the Passion, then the cross is eternally with God.

Of course, we exist in space and time, so the

---

[6] In Origen's view, Jesus Christ *always already* a human being, as well as divine, of course.

Incarnation must manifest in space and time. Because we must tell the story of the Word's Incarnation, we run the risk of imprisoning that eternal reality within the bounds of space and time.

We do not know any God besides the crucified and risen one. The cross is our lens and prism for understanding the revelation of God in Christ. The cross allows us to see the divine economy that exists in heaven, that is, in eternity. The cross allows us to "see," to understand, the spiritual nature of Christ, and through Christ, the spiritual nature of all things. We must start all theology, all speculation, all thought with Christ crucified.

Moses and all the prophets had always spoken about how the Son of Man enters His glory by suffering. Yet the glory and divinity of the Son of Man were not in fact seen until the exaltation upon the Cross.

If we try to look behind the Cross, we will not see the true God, Jesus Christ—we will see the human being called Jesus before the Passion, as if the Passion never happened. We will see Jesus only as the son of a carpenter from Nazareth. We will not contemplate the Word of God. If, on the other hand, we look through the Cross, we see the unchanging identity of the crucified One throughout His life. Jesus Christ, from His birth from the Virgin and throughout his ministry, is always the God-man.

Now the human soul is both evil and good, so we might ask how Christ can have a human soul. After all, there is no evil in Christ!

Christ's soul was so in love with righteousness, that any thought or impulse contrary to His great love was utterly destroyed. Therefore, any evil in the human soul was, in His soul, destroyed. At no time was there even a possibility of sin for Jesus.

Christ willed the good so perfectly in human nature that it was transfigured into God's nature, which is always wholly good. In this way, all human nature was healed as it was assumed into God's good will. His human nature was placed in the Word forever, like iron being placed in the fire. Being ceaselessly kindled, Christ's soul is always in union with God. Some warmth of the Word of God must have passed to all the saints, but the divine fire itself rested in Christ's soul. When a piece of iron is placed in a fire, it loses the properties of cold and hard and takes on the properties of hot and fluid, while remaining iron. This is how it is with the human nature of Jesus.

We come into being in time. However, we are to put on the identity of Jesus, the eternally begotten Son of God. Our end, which is to be a participant in the eternal liturgy in the heavenly court, is achieved through the death and resurrection in Christ. We are to enter into an eternal reality—heaven. Indeed, in a sense, we must always already be there. In time, we have not yet arrived there. But in eternity, we are there. Our life on earth is a shadow stretched out upon the earth of that heavenly reality, a shadow cast, as upon the Virgin, by the power of the Most High. Our true reality is indeed hidden with Christ in God.

The mature, perfected Christian shares in the activity of God. The whole life of such a perfected human being is one of festival and thanksgiving. We are images, or icons, of our eternal reality. This present fleshly life of death is a false life. Our end is to become true human beings. For this to happen, we must have the fullness of Christ within us. We must be filled with the Holy Spirit.

In Christ, the space of heaven and the region of earth are united. In the Eucharist, the worshipper, represented by the High Priest, enters heaven through Christ. Here, time and eternity—this world and the world to come—intersect and become one. Eternity is opened up to us on the cross, in and through the Passion of Christ.

The liturgy we experience in church is an image of the heavenly liturgy. We participate in this heavenly liturgy by taking up our cross.

In this, we participate in the passion of Christ, the One we love; and if we die with Him, we will be raised with Him in glory.

SCRIPTURE

Let us discuss how we are to understand the holy scriptures. First you must know that scripture is holy and inspired. Think how there have been countless lawgivers, teachers, and philosophers declaring that they have the truth. But their words lacked power.

Throughout the world, numerous people have abandoned their ancestral laws and gods and given themselves to the observance of the Law of Moses and to the worship of Christ. They embraced Christ's teaching with all affection, in spite of the persecution of idol worshippers. All can see that this preaching has been accepted because of the power of God and the demonstration of the Spirit. Scriptures are divine, not written with any human skill or eloquence.

The Word of God dwells among us in the scriptures, but only if we recline on His breast, as did John. We come to know the Word only when we give ourselves to Him.

However, the scriptures could not be understood until the arrival of Christ. Christ illuminated the Law of Moses with the light of truth and took away that veil which had covered the letters. Christ revealed, for everyone who believes in Him, all the good things that were hidden and buried within the scriptures. Before the revelation of Christ, we could not understand the Old Testament correctly. We needed a special lens to see the true meaning.

That lens is Christ. The Old Testament is full of enigmas and ambiguities. Those who read it without the proper explanation will benefit little. The Truth it contains is only brought to light by the cross of Christ, and only by reading it in this light do we find the Wisdom of God.

The Spirit had three aims in inspiring the scriptures. The first was to instruct human beings about themselves and their situation. The second was to conceal such matters from those who don't work to discover them, while still making the scriptures beneficial through an abundance of moral examples. The third was to weave into the narrative enough stumbling blocks and obstacles and "impossibilities" to make us aware that there is a deeper meaning to be found.

Scripture uses historical events as a medium to express spiritual truths. One meaning of scripture is fleshly—this is the depiction of historical events. But there is also a spiritual meaning to scripture. Reading scripture through the lens of Christ reveals the spiritual reality behind the historical events recorded. This is the eschatological reading: a revelation of the spiritual meaning of the stories told in scripture.

The whole scripture has a spiritual meaning, but not all of it has a bodily, or fleshly, meaning. Scripture will sometimes interweave things that did not happen, that have no historical reality; they are told only to reveal a spiritual truth.

The Apostle Paul gave us numerous examples of spiritual meanings in scripture. He says, "For it is written in the law of Moses, "You shall not muzzle an ox while it treads out the grain."" And, then, when explaining how this ought to be understood, he asked, "Is it oxen God is concerned about?"[xxiii]

Paul said that the spiritual rock, in Moses' time, was symbolic of Christ.[xxiv] Writing to the Galatians, he admonished some who read the Law yet were unaware there were symbols within, such as Abraham's two sons—one born according to the flesh and one born through promise—being symbolic of two covenants.[xxv]

Writing to the Hebrews and discussing those who are of the old covenant, Paul says they "serve the copy and shadow of the heavenly things."[xxvi]

So, when we read scripture, we must always ask ourselves whether the events within may also be figurative. The reason scripture includes certain stumbling blocks is so we will pause and ponder the spiritual meaning. The Holy Spirit took care to do this so that when those things on the surface cannot be true or useful, we will diligently search for an understanding that we believe is worthy of God and inspired by God.

For example, surely everyone can see how unreasonable it is to claim there was a first, second, and third day with evening and morning but no sun, moon, or stars! How can a first day exist without a sky?

And who is foolish enough to suppose that God, as a human gardener, planted trees in Eden and a tree of life? Could anyone really believe that there was a real tree that anyone could eat of and gain the knowledge of good and evil?

Again, when God is said to walk in paradise in the afternoon and Adam hides behind a tree, no one, I think, really doubts that these things are figurative and indicate certain mystical truths.

And Cain going out from the presence of God stirs a careful reader to seek the spiritual meaning of the presence of God, and how one can go out from it.

Think of when the scriptures mention the devil placing Jesus on a high mountain, that he might from there show Him all the kingdoms of the world and their glory. How could it have been that Jesus was led by the devil onto a high mountain, or that the devil showed to His fleshly eyes all the kingdoms of the world?

Similar things are found in the passages containing the commandments. For in the Law, Moses commanded that every male who had not been circumcised on the eighth day was to be destroyed, which is most illogical.

And anyone who has read carefully will find interwoven in the Gospels things that are not accepted as history but may hold a spiritual meaning.

But no one should suspect that *none* of the scriptural history happened, just because we suspect that *some* of it did not happen.

For who can deny that Abraham was buried in the double cave at Hebron, together with Isaac and Jacob, and that Shechem was given as a portion to Joseph, and that Jerusalem is the metropolis of Judea, in which the temple of God was built by Solomon, and innumerable other statements? For the passages that are historically true are much more numerous than those woven with a purely spiritual meaning.

For our position is that all of scripture has a

spiritual meaning, but not all of it has a bodily meaning, for there are many places where the bodily meaning proves impossible. For example, when God is said to be a consuming fire, it is not because He consumes matter. Rather, God consumes our evil thoughts, wicked actions, and desire for sin.

A spiritual interpretation of scripture shows the heavenly realities. For example, scripture provides a narrative of the bodily Israelites who descended from Adam, yet also of the spiritual Israelites—the people who followed God's law in their hearts.

The Apostle Paul reveals the spiritual meaning of Jerusalem, saying, "But the Jerusalem above is free, which is the mother of us all."[xxvii] And in another epistle, he says, "But you have come to Mount Zion and to the city of the living God, the heavenly Jerusalem, to an innumerable company of angels, to the general assembly and church of the firstborn who are registered in heaven..."[xxviii]

If, then, Israel consists of a specific race of people who perceive God and His ways, and Jerusalem is a city in heaven, it follows that the cities of Israel have as their mother the Jerusalem in heaven. Therefore, whatever is prophesied of Jerusalem, we understand as prophecy about heaven. Likewise, we understand in a spiritual manner the promises

God has given Israel. Those who are faithful will dwell in "Jerusalem" at death, that is, heaven.

Others will end up in Hades, which we read as "Egypt." There they will be in bondage to evil spirits, just as fleshly Jews were in bondage to Pharaoh. For if there are spiritual Israelites, it follows that there are also spiritual Egyptians and Babylonians. If a man is a spiritual Israelite, he is one who can see God, while a spiritual Egyptian would be one who is an adversary of God.

When the scriptures speak of those whose bodies fell in the wilderness,[xxix] the spiritual sense refers to those who have sinned and made little progress in this life. They are lost in the wilderness; that is, they are punished for their sinful lives.

When the scriptures speak of the various battles of Israel, we interpret these, too, in a spiritual way. Those who go forth to the Israelite battles fight against those enemies and adversaries whom the Father subjects to the Son at His right hand, that He may destroy every principality and power.

The treasure of divine meanings is contained within the frail vessel of the common letter. In this way we become aware of the eternal Gospel hidden from the ages and now revealed by Our Lord Jesus Christ. Sharing in the light of the Father, Son, and Holy Spirit, we obtain the benefit of the Father's nature, which is eternal. The human being is made in the image and likeness of God, but this image is not seen in the form of the body but through the attainment of virtue, particularly as a person learns to be merciful. We are called to advance from bodily things to spiritual realities.

OUR TRUE CREATION

We must distinguish between what the scriptures call "creation" and what is mere "fashioning" or "making."

"Creation" refers to what God creates from His being directly—what is full of His eternal Spirit. This is matter permeated with Logos, which acts in accordance with God's will. What we see about us now is really just a molding of dead matter, devoid of His life and Spirit. True creation is born of the Word; the other is lifeless, irrational matter governed not by Logos but by necessity.

True creation is joined to the life-giving energies of God; it is eternal, obeying His will. The matter we have now decays because God, Who is eternal, is not "in" it. To be properly called "created," the Cosmos must become full of His Spirit. When God is all in all, then true creation will have begun.

True creation is persuaded by God's beauty to "be." Wooed by His great love, it has said "Amen" and "Yes" to its creator. God's creation requires a response. Indeed, we ourselves do not truly live until we say "Amen" to God. Everything and everyone will come, in the end, to bow their knees in subjection to Christ, Who becomes "all in all" through His own subjection to God the Father. When this happens, it will be the beginning of true creation. Therefore, true reality is brought into existence at the end of time, not the beginning.

The word "apocalypse" means to reveal. It is the Christ of the Apocalypse that reveals, on the cross, the beginning of God's true creation. On the cross, Christ gives His *Amen* on behalf of man and the cosmos. This is because the true creation must give an "Amen" to God to come into full existence. The same goes for us; this life is given to us to say "yes" to God.

It may sound paradoxical, but death, particularly the death of the martyrs, shows us how true life comes into being. Christ came so that we might have life—not biological life, but spiritual life. However, death must come first. As the Psalm says, "When You take away their breath, they shall die and return again to their dust. You shall send forth Your Spirit, and they shall be created."[xxx] The movement of the work of God is always, in scripture, from death to life: "I kill and I make alive."[xxxi] The "Amen" that completes the creative work of God, making it His true faithful creation, is that given by the martyr.

Thus, we have not yet been created. Not truly. Not fully. Nor has the Cosmos really begun. First comes death, and then comes life.

Humanity is made from the dirt, but he has not yet been created in a spiritual manner, in God's own image. We are not now truly living but exist in a kind of death. True life is not biological but spiritual. God desires a true living Icon of Himself, in accord with His will.

Now, there are two creation accounts in Genesis. The first "creation" in Genesis 1 depicts our true creation as God intended, made in His image. God creates the world and all that is in it, including humankind, over the course of six days. Now, everything was made at once, but for the sake of clarity, a list of days and their events is given. This depicts God's true creation as it exists outside of time, in eternity. This is the spiritual destiny of the Cosmos, which it now strains toward. This true creation comes first in the Bible because it is the "foundation" for all things, the reason our present Cosmos exists. Of course, from our perspective in time, we see it occurring at the end of all things. But eternity exists "above" time, outside of it. And everything rises, just as Christ rose, toward that heavenly reality.

We find a second creation account in Genesis 2. Here, man is made from the dirt. This creation exists in time. This is our cosmos in its fallen state. It is "fallen" because it not does not yet meet God's true intention. It is still growing into God, just as a child is growing into an adult. However, this does not mean, as many Gnostics say, that matter is evil.

So, in scripture, our true existence comes first, in Genesis 1. Yet, in the realm of time, Genesis 2 comes first, and only at the end of time will we experience the creation of Genesis 1, which exists in eternity.

We must read scripture carefully. Notice there are two verbs used to describe the creation of humankind.

In the first story of our true eternal creation in Genesis 1, God is said to have "made" humankind—the verb is *poieô*, from whence we get the word "poetry." This is the creation of heavenly man in his spiritual existence.

In the second story in Genesis 2, God "formed" the first human from the dust of the earth. The verb used there is *plassô*, from whence we get the word "plastic." Now, that which comes from the earth is not fully created from God's energies; it is molded from earthly matter. Our bodies are made of flesh from the earth, but this matter is being transformed into the consuming fire that is God.

Note also the different verbs used in the two creation accounts. Everything else in Genesis 1 is simply spoken into existence by the words, "Let there be." The only thing said to be God's own work for which He takes counsel, human beings made in His image, is expressed by the words, "Let us make." This is the true creation of spiritual humanity with God in eternity. This is the "invisible" creation that the Holy Spirit can help us see hidden in scripture.

Thus, Genesis 1 gives us the account of creation from the perspective of the Creator, while Genesis 2 gives it from the perspective of Adam and Eve and their relationship to one another. First, comes our relationship with God; second, our relationship with one another. Only if the first relationship is good can the second be blessed.

Genesis 1 is highly symbolic. The water, for example, symbolizes man's mind. Therefore, the fish represent affections and desires that arise in the mind. Birds are heavenly impulses. The earth is the body, and the beasts and creeping creatures brought forth from the earth are carnal impulses. When scripture says we are to rule the wild beasts, understand that we are to rule over the impulses and desires of our body.

This temporal creation is only completed on the cross with Christ's final word, "It is finished," or, "It is perfected."[xxxii] Only then has the true human being, Jesus Christ, finally appeared. Jesus is the first true human being, the first-born of every creature, fully created in the Spirit, not merely made from the earth.

This is why Pilate says, "Behold the human being."[xxxiii] This is also why St. Ignatius, like many martyrs, asked on his way to martyrdom that the Romans be silent about him so that he could follow Christ in martyrdom and so "become human." For it is through death, the death of Jesus, that true spiritual life comes.

We come into this world in Adam, not in the Spirit. We will be born from the Spirit when we learn to give our "Amen" fully to God in Christ and then are raised up with him after our death. Our true beginning will occur in heaven.

Our election, which happens from the foundation of the world, is the call that brings us into being. The final end when God will be all in all transcends time; it is always there, beyond the temporal horizon, in an eternal now. This true creation happens in eternity, but from our perspective within time, we are still groaning toward this heavenly reality.

THE FALL

God's power is the source of every power carried out by his creatures, even by those who have fallen into apostasy and rebellion. God has given all rational creatures a participation in Himself, to the extent that we hold to Him in love.

However, because of free will, one person is attached to God by an ardent love, and another by a feebler and weaker love. The whole of scripture, read with spiritual eyes, is speaking about our continual falling away from God from the beginning of created time.

This affects all of Creation. The creation was subjected to futility, not willingly, but by the One who subjected it in hope,[xxxiv] so that the sun, the moon, the stars, and the angels of God might fulfill an obedient service for the world.

For the world needed to be made to fit cold souls and bodies. This world cannot have matter filled with the fiery love of God, for our bodies could not survive it. Hence, this imperfect fallen Cosmos reflects our imperfect fallen souls. This visible world was founded for those souls who would need these denser bodies because of their excessive spiritual defects.

God always intended that Christ would be incarnate, fully God and fully man, and that we would be educated in this temporal universe.

God foresaw the ways we would all fall short of His perfect intention for a perfect creation. To be made fit for eternity with Him, we would need to learn how to receive His love. He placed each person in the exact life position where he or she could conform to His will. The present Cosmos is a large schoolroom where we may be taught how to exist in His love. The world functions as a school and a hospital for our souls, where we undergo the necessary education and purification of sins. God is our compassionate teacher, physician, and father.

Because He is above time, our future lies open to God. He knows, in the words of Paul, whether each of us will be a vessel of honor or a vessel of dishonor.

However, He is not the cause! We have free will. It is we who make His knowledge true by our own choices of good or evil. Our lives are governed by God's providence but are not determined by God. God woos us with His beauty and love. He seeks to persuade us, but He will never compel us against our will.

Every rational being who turns aside from reason sins. Since all rational creatures were given free will, this freedom will be used either to make progress in imitating God or to turn away from God through neglect. Suffering and evil do not come from the will or judgement of the Creator, but from the freedom of the human will when used incorrectly.

All of mankind's desire finds fulfillment in Christ. The very nature of desire is to love God. So, Adam is to become like Christ. Christ is the archetype toward which Adam moves.

Now, our end is to enter into the eternity of God, being purged by Him as by a consuming fire. Then we will come to share in His characteristics, while remaining human, as our hearts become aflame with love.

Just so, the cooler our love for Him, the more we fall away from His image. With spiritual understanding, we see that the true Creation exists first in eternity, as the foundation. So, our beginning in time can only be thought of as a falling away from that eternal and heavenly reality.

Now I do not describe this falling away in terms of taking a body. Falling away means we fall short of being aflame with love for God. We fall by being cool. God is a consuming fire. Whenever scripture speaks of the manifestation of God in creation, it is in fiery terms (the burning bush, for instance), whereas whenever it speaks of the adverse powers and their works, it is always as "cold."

Christ has come "to cast fire upon the earth." He set Simon's and Cleopas's hearts aflame on the road to Emmaus. If our end is to be in the consuming fire that is God, transformed and sharing in the properties of that fire, then our cooling down by descending from that fire resulted in denser bodies. When we remove ourselves from God's fire, our souls cool and become ever more solid and slow, like lava cooling into black rock.

As long as our souls are plunged into the great fire of God, they are aflame with the love of God and require a spiritual body that can bear the fire of God's love. For the spiritual body is made of a kind of spiritual fire. The purpose of this world is to burn away our sins and prepare our souls for rebirth in spiritual bodies. All flesh must become fire. Whenever we successfully contemplate God, we blaze just a little brighter. When we become distracted, our heart's cool.

Salvation is the process of renewing the image of God in our inner man. It is a process of being made similar to our original prototype, which is Christ. Likeness to the Savior is our natural condition.

The image of the evil one is foreign to us by nature, but by "beholding the image of the devil," we have adopted his image. Evil is not a real substance, for only the good is real. Thus, evil is the absence of good, as cold is the absence of heat.

We assume a likeness to the evil one whenever our soul turns toward the flesh and the desires of the flesh. This causes an unnatural union between the soul and the flesh. This union is "adulterous" and unfruitful. For our true Bridegroom is Christ, and a fruitful marriage is union to Him only.

By beholding the image of God, man can return to His likeness. Thus, we must labor to contemplate Him. There is a difference between acting like Him and becoming like Him. By Christ's Incarnation, His nature can become our nature by grace. We must participate, in prayer and worship, in the life-giving energies of God.

So, we have "descended" or been "thrown down" into this world from our high calling, which caused us to be fashioned from irrational dust subject to decay and to our own fallen will.

Be careful; we must not think of ourselves as pre-existing in the sense of time. We did not exist before this world's beginning in any temporal sense. We cannot use the word "before" when it comes to things outside of time. Yet, our election is prior to our being fashioned from the dust of the earth.

ESCHATOLOGY

Death was not created by God, and one day it will be destroyed. Its hostile purpose will come to an end. It will not cause anything to perish; rather it will be used to change things in accordance with the will of God.

Evil, like death, was not made by God. Just as darkness is not a thing in itself, but simply the absence of light, so evil is only the absence of good. Evil, therefore, has no being. Only God is Being. If God will be "all in all,"[xxxv] then evil, will be found no more.

As long as we stick to God and hold to the One who truly Is, then we truly exist. When we go far from God and adhere to evil we, in a sense, become non-being. This is not a vanishing of the soul, but spiritual death.

The fires of judgment will destroy, not sinners, but their evil thoughts. Thanks to the Incarnation and resurrection of Christ, the final vanishing of evil from all humans will be able to take place. His death produced the destruction of evil and the devil.

Every being may be restored to oneness with God when He is "all in all." However, this will not happen in a moment. It will happen slowly, through innumerable aeons[7] of

---

[7] Ages.

indefinite duration in the afterlife. God takes care of all. His providential care mainly takes the form of illumination, instruction, and correction, according to the needs of each individual. Some may advance in love for God with a faster rhythm; others may lag a long distance behind. Eventually those aeons will be no more, and all will be reconciled with God. Then the last enemy, Death, will be destroyed.[xxxvi]

This will not be against our free will. By gradual education, we will all freely choose to become one with God as we learn to love God. For if all the factors St. Paul listed[xxxvii] cannot separate us from God's love, still less will our free will be able to separate us from God's love! The aeons in the afterlife will offer time to become purified, illuminated, and voluntarily submitted to God. This is against the Stoics and Gnostics, who say we have no free will and that everything is determined.

Our destiny is theosis.[8] We will become divinized in the likeness of Him who created us. The Holy Apostle John says we will be like Him and see Him as He is.[xxxviii] You who follow Christ will no longer be humans, but, according to Christ's teaching, will be like angels of God. The Lord quotes, "I said, "You are gods, And you are

---

[8] Deification; likeness to or union with God.

all sons of the Most High."[xxxix]

In the eternal restoration, no one will fall again. For the perfection of love reached in the very end will allow no falls, yet rational creatures will keep their free will.

What will prevent the free will from falling again into sin? The Apostle tells us when he says in 1 Corinthians 13 that love never fails. Love is greater than faith and hope because it is the only thing that will prevent all sin. For, if the soul has reached such a degree of perfection as to love God with all its heart, with all its mind, and with all its forces, and its neighbor as much as itself, what room will be left for sin?

Love could not prevent Satan's or Adam's fall because their falls occurred before the manifestation of Christ's love. The power and effectiveness of Christ's death are so great as to set right all past, present, and future aeons. In the end, all rational creatures will voluntarily hold to God in so strong a love that they will never fall again, as they could at the beginning. Indeed, one for whom God is "all things" no longer desires to eat the fruit of the tree of the knowledge of good and evil.

Evil, I believe, is chosen because it is mistaken for a good, due to insufficient knowledge or a clouding of the mind. Sin is rightly called ignorance. This is why instruction and illumination are vital to restoration. The angels and saints are always imparting wisdom to come to knowledge of God.

Freedom is about knowledge. The more a person knows, the more rational and informed their choices become. This is the sentiment behind John 8:32, "And you shall know the truth, and the truth shall make you free," as well as Luke 23:34, "Then Jesus said, "Father forgive them, for they do not know what they do."" Sin is not ill will but rather ignorance or an error of judgment. It is an evil mistaken for a good and therefore needs correction rather than punishment. This restoration of our rationality is one key to our freedom. Thus, our salvation is, in part, learning to choose the good. In my opinion, the meaning of the 'outer darkness' in scripture is not a dark atmosphere but rather the darkness of profound ignorance, alien to every glimmer of reason or understanding.

Of course, human intention alone is incapable of any good. A human being would never by himself be able to conquer an opposing power, unless he had the benefit of divine assistance. The same can be said of the opposite direction. The first movement towards self-indulgence is our own will, but then the hostile powers seize the opportunity and press hard to extend our sins. We human beings provide the occasions and beginnings of sins, while hostile powers spread them far and wide.

Once we suffer something unpleasant, the demons try to arouse us either to great anger, excessive sorrow, or the depths of despair. They try to induce us, when we are wearied, to make complaints against God. We may then become weak in faith, hopeless, or driven to abandon the truth and think impiously about God.

The demons' influence is most harmful. Evil spirits either possess the mind so that the mind understands nothing at all, or they deprave the soul by hostile suggestions and evil persuasions.

On the other hand, someone receives the energy and work of a good spirit when he is moved to good and inspired towards divine things. The holy angels spurred the prophets towards better things. Yet it remained within their will and judgement whether or not to follow the encouragement. Hence, our cooperation is required.

There are remedies available to us Christians for our sins: baptism, almsgiving, forgiveness, the conversion of a sinner, and an abundance of charity. There is also the hard way of affliction, tears, mortification of the flesh, and fasting. And, through misfortunes, we are tested, disciplined, and corrected.

When the soul has accumulated sins, at the right time the evils are set aflame to correction. The conscience becomes agitated and pierced and becomes its own accuser and witness.

The otherworldly "punishment" of sinners in the afterlife is healing, educational, and purifying. It is an intense pain when the soul is found outside of the order, connection, and harmony it was created for. For Christ is a physician of souls Whose aim is to heal all rational souls with the therapy that comes from the Logos, to make them friends of God. All will pass through the purifying fire, and the duration of each one's time in it will be equal to his sins. Thus, we say this fire is a spiritual reality signifying the state of our closeness or alienation from God.

Yet the divine will insist on the cleansing of every soul, no matter how defiled it has become. God is said in scripture to kill and destroy, but He only does so in order to remake creatures better. Resurrection is always His strategy.

I interpret the concept of "eternal fire" to mean a fire appropriate to the age rather than an everlasting flame. The soul during purification might continue in its great cosmic ascent, from age to age, across the great span of God's plan of salvation, until finally arriving at the end of all ages in full communion with God. This salvation depends on Christ's Incarnation, death, and resurrection, as well as His healing work as Physician and His instructive activity as Logos. Christ's sacrifice, though it took place once, had the power of healing and rectifying all rational creatures in all aeons. We also say that Christ is the savior and offering for the entire Cosmos. Through the resurrection, the whole creation was restored to God.

The blood of Christ was a ransom paid to Satan, whose prisoners we become when we allow his image to expel the image of God in our souls. Yet Satan is never master of our wills. We are taught by Christ to suppress evil thoughts and refrain from sin. Therefore, let us contemplate unceasingly Christ, the image of God, so as to be transformed into His likeness.

Satan himself, I think, may be saved. Not as Satan, for nothing can oppose God in eternity when He is all in all. Rather, every sinful aspect of Satan will be purged from his being, until only his original goodness is left. For God is not the author of death or evil. Of course, it is possible that only the demons will be saved and that the devil himself, so corrupted in sin, can never be destined for blessedness. Yet we must allow that God could *in theory* save Satan, even if he is not in fact destined for salvation. Then again, perhaps some or all of the demons will not be saved at all, for I am uncertain as to whether those cast "into outer darkness"[xl] will remain there forever or will one day be released. This is a matter we can only speculate on with great uncertainty. It does not seem to me safe to judge; I have no knowledge, since nothing is written on the subject.

Regarding both the salvation of Satan and the salvation of all, we must not discuss these things with the immature Christian for fear of causing moral laxity. These things are only for the spiritually advanced. These are issues we may discuss but not define.

Another speculation proper only for those mature Christians is the spiritual meaning of the Second Coming of our Lord. Christ's "Second Coming" is not simply a return on the clouds at the end of days, but a coming in glory to those who want to embrace him more perfectly right now. So, His promised Second Coming is fulfilled already in the souls of those who ascend to communion with Christ.

We must read the mystical meaning of the end-time events in scripture. The famine in Matthew 24:7 symbolizes the hunger that the lover of Christ has for the depths of scriptural mysteries. The clouds on which the coming Lord will be enthroned are the writings of the prophets and apostles. The "heavens" where the Son of Man gathers his elect are the sacred books of the church. The last trumpets of the angels are the gospel as it has been proclaimed throughout the world. Thus, we must avoid too literal a sense but also not fall into the opposite gnostic tendency to deny the real sense of God's plan unfolding within history.

The earth will pass away, but its passing away is a renewal, not a destruction. This new earth, and indeed all matter in the new Creation, will not be immaterial, as the Gnostics teach, but will be a material shining with God's light.

Now, what does it mean to be "in Christ?" We cannot say. I can only give you the three most common speculations on the subject.

Some say the afterlife will be very similar to our existence now. Some say there will be some kind of absorption into Christ. Finally, some say there will be a radical transformation of all things into some purely spiritual nature. The reader is invited to discover the truest and best of these three ideas.

I think we will be given spiritual bodies patterned after our previous bodies (but not made of the same atoms) that reflect the states of our souls. For the soul gives the body unity and identity even now and will do so for the risen body later.

I say our bodies in the afterlife will be glorified bodies aflame with God's spirit. When we die, our bodies will disintegrate and be dissolved back into the earth. But what is sown will rise in power and glory, as a spiritual body.

As created beings embodied in matter, we are called to become one and eternal with God. We are called to be purged of our vices and passions by the consuming fire that is God. We are called to become the very temple of God Himself, our matter transformed by the power of God. This is our final destination at the end of all ages. However, the resurrection is a power experienced already in part.

The final Resurrection of the dead is not merely a matter of an individual soul but about the mystery of the church drawn back into total communion with God as its source. The faithful will radiate as one body like a single sun. On that final day, when God is all in all, our separateness will also come to an end, in a perfection of communion and unity.

The saints have an incomparably more vital communion with the Logos because of their clarified state of vision yet are still in communion with the earthly church. Their prayers, especially the powerful intercessions of the martyred saints, collaborate in Christ's ongoing work to purify and raise up spiritual intelligence on Earth.

If there is anyone who is able to discover something better and to confirm what he says by clearer statements from the holy scriptures, let those accounts be received rather than mine. In Christ, be blessed.

ABOUT JONATHAN

Jonathan McCormack is a writer and artist. His writings have been published in various journals, and his art has been featured in the journal Jesus the Imagination and elsewhere. He is working out his salvation in fear and trembling as an Orthodox Christian in New York. He accepts commissions at JonathanMcCormack.com.

[i] Origen. *On First Principles: A Reader's Edition*. Translated by John Behr. New York, NY: Oxford University Press, 2019.

[ii] Tzamalikos Panagiōtēs. *Origen: Philosophy of History and Eschatology*. Leiden: Brill, 2007.

[iii] Eusebius, and Paul L. Maier. *Eusebius: The Church History*. Grand Rapids, MI: Kregel , 1999.

[iv] Schaff, Philip. "Prefaces to Jerome's Early Works." In *The Church Fathers. The Complete Ante-Nicene & Nicene and Post-Nicene Church Fathers Collection*. London: Catholic Way Publishing, 2014. Kindle edition.

[v] St. Gregory of Nazianzus, and St. Basil of Caesarea. *The Philocalia of Origen*. Translated by George Lewis. Aeterna Press, 2014.

[vi] McGuckin, John Anthony. *St Gregory of Nazianzus: An Intellectual Biography*. Crestwood, NY: St Vladimir's Seminary Press, 2011.

[vii] Balthasar, Hans Urs von. *Origen, Spirit and Fire: A Thematic Anthology of His Writings*. Translated by Robert J. Daly. Washington, D.C.: Catholic University of America Press, 2001.

[viii] Tanner, Norman P. *Decrees of the Ecumenical Councils*. Washington, D. C.: Georgetown University Press, 1990.

[ix] Ware, Kallistos. *The Inner Kingdom*. Crestwood, NY: St. Vladimir's Seminary Press, 2001.

[x] McGuckin, John Anthony. *The Path of Christianity: The First Thousand Years*. Downers Grove, IL: An Imprint of InterVarsity Press, 2017.

[xi] Harl, Marguerite "La pre-existence des âmes dans l'oeuvre d'Origène", Origeniana Quarta, ed. by L. Lies, 257. Innsbruck: Tyrolia-Verlag, 1987.

[xii] Edwards, Mark Julian. *Origen Against Plato*. New York, NY: Routledge, 2018.

[xiii] Tzamalikos Panagiōtēs. *Origen: Philosophy of History and Eschatology*. Leiden: Brill, 2007.

[xiv] Hart, David Bentley. Review of *On First Principles*, by Origen. *Journal of Orthodox Christian Studies* 3, no. 1 (2020): 103-107. doi:10.1353/joc.2020.0008.

[xv] Harl, Marguerite "La pre-existence des âmes dans l'oeuvre

d'Origène", Origeniana Quarta, ed. by L. Lies, 257. Innsbruck: Tyrolia-Verlag, 1987.

[xvi] St. Pamphilus. *Apology for Origen: With the Letter of Rufinus on the Falsification of the Books of Origen*. Translated by Thomas P. Scheck. Washington, D.C.: Catholic University of America Press, 2010.

[xvii] John of Damascus. *An Exposition of the Orthodox Faith*, 15. 11-13

[xviii] Hart, David Bentley. "Final Thoughts on the Last Things: Reflections on New Testament Eschatology, Part Seven." Leaves in the Wind. Substack, May 23, 2022. https://davidbentleyhart.substack.com/.

[xix] Dan R. Schlesinger, "Did Origen teach reincarnation? A response to neo-Gnostic theories of Christian reincarnation with particular reference to Origen and to the Second Council of Constantinople (553)," MPhil(R) thesis, (University of Glasgow, 2016).

[xx] 1 Cor. 15:28

[xxi] Gregory of Nyssa. *Homilies on the Song of Songs*. Translated by Richard A Norris. Society of Biblical Literature, 2012.

[xxii] Heb. 1:2

[xxiii] 1 Cor. 9:9-10, OSB

[xxiv] 1 Cor. 10:4, OSB

[xxv] Gal. 4:21-24, OSB

[xxvi] Heb. 8:5, OSB

[xxvii] Gal. 4:26, OSB

[xxviii] Heb. 12:22-23

[xxix] Heb. 3:17

[xxx] Psalm 103(104):29-30, OSB

[xxxi] Deut. 32:39

[xxxii] John 19:30

[xxxiii] John 19:5

[xxxiv] Rom. 8:20

[xxxv] 1 Cor. 15:28

[xxxvi] 1 Cor. 15: 25-26

[xxxvii] Rom. 8:35-39

[xxxviii] 1 John 3:2

xxxix Psalm 81(82):6 OSB
xl Matthew 22:13 OSB

* 9 7 9 8 3 5 6 8 6 4 5 0 6 *